For Patty + Patrick
Merry Aloha!
~Bill

D0532007

HAWAI‘I'S
Gathering
PLACE

AN ISLAND TREASURES BOOK

CHERYL CHEE TSUTSUMI
photographs by
VERONICA CARMONA

ISLAND HERITAGE
PUBLISHING

HAWAII'S Gathering PLACE
THE ISLAND OF O'AHU

PRECEDING PAGES:

Young dancers revive the beauty and drama of *kahiko* (ancient) Hawaiian dances in a high school hula competition, King Samuel Wilder Intermediate School, Kāneʻohe.

RIGHT:

*W*aikiki's glittering skyline lightens the somber mood of night.

Published and distributed by
ISLAND HERITAGE PUBLISHING

ISBN 0-89610-387-0

Address orders and correspondence to:

 ISLAND HERITAGE™
P U B L I S H I N G
94-411 Kōʻaki Street
Waipahu, Hawaiʻi 96797
Orders: 800-468-2800
Information: 808-564-8800
Fax: 808-564-8877
islandheritage.com

Printed in Hong Kong
Second edition, second printing, 2005

PROJECT MANAGER: VIRGINIA WAGEMAN
DESIGNED BY JIM WAGEMAN

Contents

Welcome
TO O'AHU

O'AHU'S NICKNAME IS "THE GATHERING PLACE," and indeed it is—for culture, for entertainment, for education, for dining, for shopping, for business, for history. A cosmopolitan population of more than 870,000 (74 percent of the state's population) resides on this 597-square-mile swatch of the tropics, which boasts an intriguing blend of sophistication and down-home charm, high energy and laid-backness.

Much of O'ahu's incredible past is shared through its attractions. In 1795 Kamehameha the Great's quest to wrest control of the island from King Kalanikūpule ended at the soaring cliffs of Nu'uanu. In what proved to be the final, decisive battle, Kamehameha's warriors drove the forces of Kalanikūpule to the top of the valley and over the edge of the steep precipice onto the jagged rocks below. Few stories in Hawaiian history are as dramatic as this—or as the view of windward O'ahu that's revealed at the two-thousand-foot-high Nu'uanu Pali lookout.

On Kamehameha Day, June 11, Islanders drape the statue of the great warrior king in downtown Honolulu with eighteen-foot leis to celebrate his birthday.

From the Pali lookout, sightseers admire a panoramic view of windward O'ahu and the majestic Ko'olau Mountain Range.

The world-renowned Bishop Museum was established in 1889 by Charles Reed Bishop in honor of his wife, Princess Bernice Pauahi Bishop, great-granddaughter of Kamehameha the Great and the last direct descendant of the Kamehameha line. Feather helmets and capes that once belonged to royalty, handsome koa wood calabashes, and ancient Hawaiian weapons and hula implements occupy a particularly esteemed place in the museum's collection of priceless treasures.

In February 1845 Kamehameha III moved the seat of government from Lahaina, Maui, to the port of Honolulu on O'ahu, which was rapidly establishing itself as the center of commerce in the kingdom. In subsequent decades, while Hawai'i's form of government changed from absolute monarchy to constitutional monarchy to annexation by the United States to U.S. territory to U.S. state, Honolulu never relinquished its role as the Islands' political, economic, and cultural hub.

On the outskirts of Greater Honolulu, Pearl Harbor remains the focal point of an important chapter in American history. On Sunday morning, December 7, 1941, Japanese warplanes roared over Pearl Harbor, dropping bombs on the U.S. Navy's

Named for a Hawaiian princess, Bishop Museum boasts the world's finest collection of natural and historical artifacts from Hawai'i and the Pacific.

FACING PAGE:
Mānoa Falls lies at the end of an easy, though often muddy, trail bordered by guava and mountain apple trees and fragrant stands of wild ginger.

mighty Pacific fleet, which lay peacefully at anchor. That attack propelled America into World War II, which was to drag on for nearly four long years.

Today Pearl Harbor is home to the two battleships that have come to symbolize the beginning and the end of the war—the USS *Arizona*, which sunk in the 1941 bombing and now rests beneath a stately white memorial that revenues from Elvis Presley's 1961 Honolulu concert helped to build, and the USS *Missouri*, where the treaty ending World War II was signed on September 2, 1945.

Beyond Honolulu, O'ahu is miraculously transformed. Within sixty minutes of the city skyline you can snorkel within the horseshoe-shaped rim of an eroded volcanic crater; cruise in a glider plane kept aloft by brisk trades; surf the most famous waves in the world; kayak to islets with curious names like Chinaman's Hat and Goat Island; and hike into secluded rain forests where only birdsong stirs the stillness.

These are just a few vignettes of an enchanting destination that mesmerizes even those who've lived there all their lives. At once rustic and refined, serene and spirited, O'ahu is the island where people love to gather.

Honolulu

Founded by New England missionaries in 1841, Punahou is one of Hawai'i's oldest and most prestigious private schools.

Downtown Honolulu's skyscrapers dwarf ten-story Aloha Tower (off center, near the bow of the ocean liner), which was the tallest building in the city when it was dedicated in 1926.

Drought plagued all of O'ahu. The heavens had not wept for months. Without water, gardens wilted, and food was scarce.

An old man named Mūkākā and his wife, Kealoha, lived in Mānoa Valley. This was a very hard time for them, for each day Mūkākā had to hike far up into the valley to gather ti roots and ferns for their meals. Meanwhile, Kealoha traversed a long rough trail to Kamō'ili'ili to fill her water gourds at one of the few springs that still flowed.

One day in particular, the journey seemed more difficult than ever. Though Kealoha rested for a spell, she could not shake off her fatigue. When she finally reached home, Mūkākā was preparing the evening meal, but Kealoha was too exhausted to eat. Instead, she lay down on lau hala (pandanus leaf) mats and cried herself to sleep.

In a dream, a man appeared beside her. "Why are you crying?" he asked.

"Because I am so tired," Kealoha replied. "Every day I must walk all

Punahou School, the largest independent school in the United States, now stands near the spot where Mūkākā discovered the life-sustaining spring, *ka puna hou*, that ended the drought in Mānoa Valley. Inspired by this legend, Punahou's seal is a *hala* tree with two taro leaves floating in the water beneath it.

Technically, the City and County of Honolulu encompasses the entire island of O'ahu, but Greater Honolulu is usually defined as the area loosely bordered by Pearl Harbor to the west, Kāhala to the east, Nu'uanu to the north, and Ala Moana to the south. Sheltered within these boundaries is a wealth of natural, cultural, and historical treasures, including Punahou School, which was founded in 1841 by Congregationalist missionaries.

With its imposing skyscrapers, endless streams of

the way to Kamō'ili'ili to get water. The trip is hot and dusty, and I no longer have the energy to do it."

"You don't have to do it anymore," the man told her. "Close by your house a spring gurgles under the hala tree. You may fill your gourds there." Then he was gone.

The next morning, Kealoha told her husband about her dream. "It can't be true," Mūkākā scoffed. "How can there be water anywhere in the parched earth that surrounds us?"

When he left, Kealoha looked at the ground beneath the hala tree by their hale (house). It was indeed dry and hard. Mūkākā was right; there couldn't possibly be any water there.

That night Mūkākā dreamed a man was standing by his sleeping mats. "There is a spring under the hala tree that grows beside your house," the man said. "Catch red fish, wrap them in ti leaves, heat the imu (underground oven), and cook the fish. Make an offering to the gods and ask for strength to pull up the tree. When you do, you will find the spring."

When Mūkākā awoke, he knew he had to follow the man's instructions. With the help of a friend, he caught and prepared red fish. He and his friend offered some of the fish to the gods and ate the rest. Then the two men went to the hala tree and tried to uproot it.

Both grasped the tree and pulled with all their might, until perspiration

Over 14,000 coral blocks quarried from offshore reefs were used to construct stately Kawaiaha'o Church.

Completed in 1882 at a cost of $360,000, 'Iolani Palace was the first building in Honolulu to be equipped with electricity. It also beat the White House and Buckingham Palace in this regard!

traffic, and packs of well-dressed executives, the core of downtown Honolulu mirrors any modern metropolis. But just a few blocks away, the past beckons: here are 'Iolani Palace, the residence of King Kalākaua and Queen Lili'uokalani, Hawai'i's last two reigning monarchs; the Mission Houses Museum, headquarters of the first contingent of Christian missionaries in Hawai'i; Kawaiaha'o Church, which

has offered Sunday services in the Hawaiian language since 1842; and exotic Chinatown, with its open-air fish and produce markets, acupuncture clinics, herb shops, noodle factories, dim sum parlors, and Buddhist and Taoist temples, where smoldering joss sticks emit mesmerizing swirls of incense-laden smoke before dignified golden images.

ran in little rivers down their faces and bodies. Finally, the earth released the tree, and they saw a bit of moisture in the hole where it once stood. Mūkākā worked his digging stick into the soil and water spurted out. He dug deeper, and out gushed more water.

Watching gleefully, Kealoha exclaimed, "Ka puna hou! *The new spring!"*

As it turned out, the spring yielded enough precious water to rejuvenate the entire village. The people planted taro and breadfruit and bananas and sweet potatoes. They built fishponds and kept them well stocked. Thanks to the gods and ka puna hou, *life was again good.*

*K*amehameha Day festivities include performances by *keiki* (children) before the lei-bedecked statue of the revered king, who is credited with uniting the Hawaiian Islands under one rule.

Honolulu exudes an engaging vivacity. There's something exciting, something entertaining, going on all the time in this dynamic cosmopolitan city—carnivals, craft fairs, luaus, parades, sports events, concerts, ethnic festivals, plays, dance performances, and more. In short, Hawai'i's capital offers every diversion imaginable.

Shopaholics converge at fifty-acre Ala Moana Shopping Center, which, with over 230 stores, restaurants, and services, holds the distinction of being one of the largest open-air malls in the world. A recently completed renovation endowed the center with a new upper level of shops, fresh landscaping, a spruced-up stage for concerts and other performances, and an expanded and enhanced international food court.

Even those desiring to escape the hustle and bustle will find peaceful, pretty oases within the city limits. Softening the hard, linear face of urban Honolulu are expansive parks, beautiful gardens, and mountain trails that wind their way deep into the heart of Mother Nature.

*L*avishly decorated floats carrying graceful hula dancers captivate crowds watching the Kamehameha Day Parade.

*R*iders in the parade's mounted *pā'ū* units reflect the ethnic diversity of O'ahu. *Pā'ū* refers to the female riders' costume—a long, full, split skirt that flows gracefully over the sides of their horses. More than a century ago, the *pā'ū* was the popular riding habit of Hawaiian women. It was originally worn as an outer garment to protect the ladies' beautiful dresses from dust, wind, and rain.

*H*awai'i's state
seal and motto
embellish the entry
gate of 'Iolani
Palace. *"Ua mau ke
ea o ka 'āina i ka
pono"* translates
as "The life of the
land is perpetuated
in righteousness."

*A*n imposing statue
of Kamehameha I
greets visitors to
Ali'iolani Hale,
the State Judiciary
Building.

FACING PAGE,
FAR RIGHT:

*C*hinatown vendors peddle fresh produce, meat, and fish at reasonable prices. Herb shops (facing page) stock exotic remedies for everything from indigestion to insomnia.

*D*octor Sun Yat-sen, first president of the Republic of China (Taiwan), was educated at ʻIolani and Punahou schools in Honolulu. A bronze statue of the Chinese statesman stands near the corner of River and Beretania streets.

*C*olorful festivals celebrate Hawai'i's rainbow of cultures. The traditional Chinese lion dance is performed during the Narcissus Festival (facing page). On this page are vignettes from the Aloha Festivals Floral Parade, the Pan Pacific Matsuri in Hawai'i Festival, and the Lantern Festival.

FAR LEFT:

*A*rchitects designed the State Capitol as a metaphor for Hawai'i: the pillars represent palm trees, the reflecting pool symbolizes the sea, and the cone-shaped rooms of the State Legislature mirror the shape of the Islands' volca-noes. An eternal flame burns in the copper and bronze sculpture by Bumpei Akaji, which is ded-icated to the people of Hawai'i who have served in the U.S. armed forces.

A statue of Father Damien de Veuster by Marisol Escobar stands at the Capi-tol's entrance.

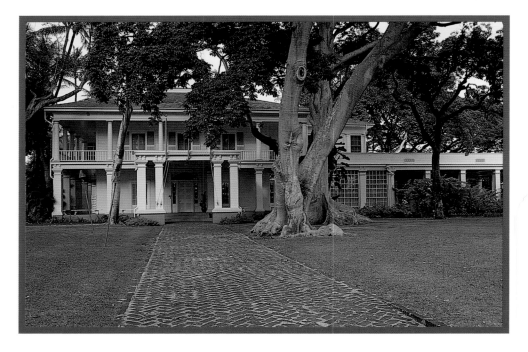

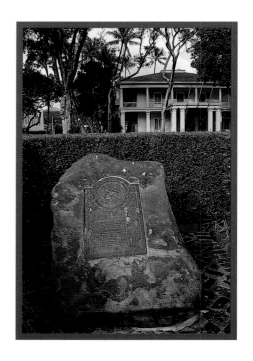

FACING PAGE,
CLOCKWISE FROM
TOP LEFT:

*I*olani Barracks
housed the Royal
Household Guards;
Hawai'i's governor
lives in Washington
Place, the former
home of Queen
Lili'uokalani; a
statue of Lili'uoka-
lani is near the State
Capitol; a plaque
at Washington
Place commemo-
rates Lili'uokalani
and her most
famous musical
composition, "Aloha
'Oe"; Mission
Houses Museum
showcases early
missionary life.

*A*loha Tower is the
centerpiece of a
bustling shopping,
dining, and enter-
tainment center.

LEFT:
*B*ishop Museum's Family Sunday promises Island-style fun.

CLOCKWISE FROM TOP LEFT:
*B*ishop Museum's Hawaiian Hall; *Falls of Clyde*, the only fully rigged, four-masted ship afloat; courtyard at the Honolulu Academy of Arts with sculpture by Jacques Lipchitz; Queen Emma and King Kamehameha IV enjoyed vacationing at this Nu'uanu retreat, now known as Queen Emma Summer Palace.

Lush tropical land-scaping and koi-filled ponds are key elements of Ala Moana Shopping Center's new look.

The Hawai'i Convention Center entices meeting and incentive groups with state-of-the-art facilities, including 200,000 square feet of exhibition space, nearly 150,000 square feet of meet-ing space, and a 36,000-square-foot ballroom.

*E*stablished in 1909, the University of Hawai'i's Mānoa campus is the largest in its statewide system.

*F*lowers are a blooming business on King Street, less than a mile from the university's Mānoa campus.

*T*he National Memorial Cemetery of the Pacific (Punchbowl) is the final resting place of over 35,000 men and women who fought in World War II and the Korean and Vietnam wars.

*T*he *Arizona* Memorial (above) and the USS *Missouri* (right) symbolize the beginning and end of World War II.

East O'ahu

PEACEFULNESS AND PIZZAZZ

There once were two handsome and powerful chiefs, Chief Koko and Chief Hana, who excelled in the sport of uma, or hand wrestling. In this ancient game, opponents lie with their stomachs to the ground, their arms locked and their hands clasped. In a sure test of strength and endurance, each tries to force the other's hand to the ground.

Both chiefs adored the beautiful Keohinani and declared their desire to marry her. But Keohinani loved both men and though she gave much thought to each proposal, she could not decide which to accept. She suggested they engage in a game of uma to determine who might be the nobler suitor; she would marry the winner.

After receiving blessings from Keohinani's father, Keanamo'o, the contest began, with the two illustrious chiefs lying on the ground, tightly gripping each other's hands. All day they sized up each other, trying to find

A two-thousand-foot-long crescent of golden sand borders cobalt blue Hanauma Bay, a popular snorkeling site that draws about 3,000 visitors per day. Designated a Marine Life Conservation District in 1967, it harbors about 100 different species of tropical fish. Visitors are encouraged to learn about and protect this nature preserve while they enjoy its beauty. To that end, a $13-million Marine Education Center, including a state-of-the-art theater and interactive exhibits, opened at the bay in August 2002.

Once you round the eastern curve of O'ahu and enter Waimānalo, the temperature appears to drop a few degrees and the scenery shifts from warm and dry to cool and green. The Ko'olau Mountains begin their spectacular thirty-mile march northward here,

weaknesses either in ability or strategy. Hours passed, and the points remained even; they appeared to be opponents of equal vigor and perseverance.

Evening approached, and the score was still tied. Neither of the two chiefs was willing to give up, and Keohinani realized she was the only one who could stop the match before both men became ill from exhaustion. She walked to a place beside a nearby bay and asked her ancestral guardians to transform her into a hill so that both Chief Koko and Chief Hana would be able to admire her beauty and innocence for the rest of their lives.

Pleased with his daughter's humble decision, Keanamo'o also turned himself into a hill overlooking the picturesque bay, which is now known as Hanauma, or hand-wrestling bay. The ridges of the two hills intertwine, reminding viewers of the strong locked arms of Chief Koko and Chief Hana as they vied for the hand of the lovely Keohinani.

Friendly dolphins welcome visitors to Sea Life Park.

Rising 760 feet above sea level, Diamond Head anchors the eastern end of Waikīkī. Scientists estimate the extinct volcano to be 500,000 years old.

dwarfing the modest homes, ranches, farms, and orchards that nestle at their base.

Just past Makapu'u Point, Sea Life Park unravels some of the mysteries of the Pacific Ocean and its fascinating inhabitants. Highlights of this popular marine attraction include interactive dolphin training sessions; shows starring *akamai* (smart) seals, whales, and dolphins; and the exhilarating Seawalker program, which enables wet suit–clad participants to get face-to-fin with tropical fish, sea turtles, manta rays, and perhaps even a shark or two as they descend twenty feet into a 300,000-gallon tank that recreates life in a Hawaiian reef.

Anchoring the other end of East O'ahu, Waikīkī provides a lively contrast to rustic Waimānalo. Packed within this sophisticated seaside resort, which measures just one-half mile wide and two miles long, are award-winning hotels, elegant

FROM LEFT:

*E*ntertaining options in Waikīkī include concerts at the Waikīkī Shell (the popular Brothers Cazimero are spotlighted here), cruises featuring

shops, first-class restaurants, and revues that rival the best Las Vegas has to offer in terms of drama and glitz. The smooth, cream-colored beaches of Waikīkī—Hawai'i's most famous ribbons of sand— are the perfect places to dally and daydream.

Hi'iaka, the younger sister of the volcano goddess Pele, because she thought its silhouette bore a strong resemblance to the fish.

O'ahu's glittering Gold Coast encompasses some of the most expensive real estate in the Islands. The

Polynesian shows aboard the *Star of Honolulu,* and the King's Jubilee at the Hilton Hawaiian Village.

*D*iamond Head surveys a perfect day in Waikīkī.

Standing guard over it all is landmark Diamond Head, so called when nineteenth-century sailors found calcite crystals sparkling on its slopes and mistook them for diamonds. Legend says that the extinct volcano's Hawaiian name, Lē'ahi, meaning brow of the *'ahi,* or yellow-fin tuna, was bestowed by

palatial estates of high-powered executives, multi-millionaire entrepreneurs, and Hollywood stars embellish the southeastern shoreline for three miles, from the foot of Diamond Head to Kāhala. Poised and refined, this neighborhood is the epitome of high living, Hawaiian style.

LEFT:

*C*anoe paddling and sailing get water lovers' adrenaline pumping.

*T*his statue on Waikīkī Beach honors famed beachboy Duke Kahanamoku, who won gold medals in swimming at the 1912 and 1920 Olympics.

RIGHT:

*O*pened in 1927, the elegant Royal Hawaiian has been nicknamed the "Pink Palace."

FACING PAGE
AND ABOVE:

*S*taged at the
Waikīkī Shell,
the Kodak Hula
Show has been
thrilling audiences
since 1937.

RIGHT:

*H*ula dancers
perform seaside
at the Sheraton
Waikīkī.

*I*ntriguing creatures
on land and in
the sea inhabit
the Honolulu Zoo
and the Waikīkī

Aquarium. Both
attractions offer
year-round educa-
tional programs
for adults and
youngsters.

Sunset heats the sky as a fisherman casts his net at Kawaikuʻi Beach Park and paddlers practice their strokes at Maunalua Bay.

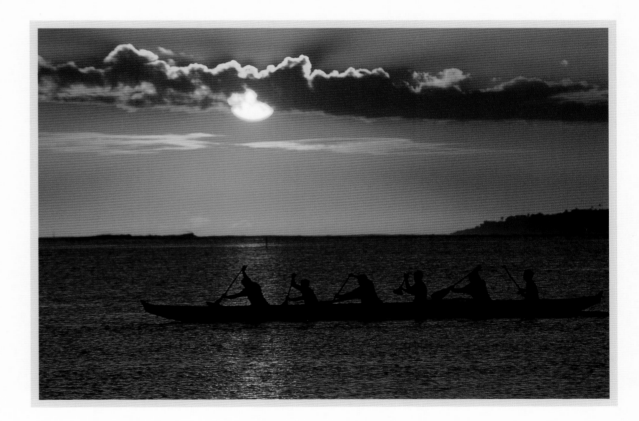

A full moon over Koko Head imbues this image with a mystical aura.

*H*ikers pause to enjoy the view along the Hawaiʻi Loa Ridge Trail.

*B*lessed with a beautiful beach, shallow shoreline waters, and abundant marine life, Hanauma Bay is a wonderful choice for swimming, snorkeling, and people watching.

FAR LEFT:
*O*nly expert swimmers should venture into the often turbulent waters of Sandy Beach.

A rainbow pierces the rocky coast below Koko Head.

*K*oko Crater harbors a 60-acre botanical garden blooming with succulents, cacti, and other species of dryland plants.

*L*ava cliffs the color
of slate meet the
brilliant turquoise
of the sea along this
scenic stretch of
southeastern Oʻahu.

*D*aring surfers
challenge the roil-
ing waves near the
Hālona Blow Hole.

Makapuʻu Point, Oʻahu's easternmost landmark, over-looks Makapuʻu Beach, Hawaiʻi's most famous bodysurfing spot.

A winding one-mile trail leads to a 646-foot bluff where the Makapuʻu Light-house is perched.

Floating off Makapuʻu Beach, 67-acre Mānana islet, popularly known as Rabbit Island, is protected as a sanctuary for seabirds.

The lamp at the Makapuʻu Light-house is a mere flicker of candle-light compared with the luminosity of the full moon.

Twilight paints the sky at Makapuʻu with broad strokes of pink and lavender.

*P*lump sea lions play in their sun-dappled pool at Sea Life Park.

*F*rom December through April, Sandy Beach offers front-row seats to continuous shows starring humpback whales that migrate to the Islands from chilly Alaskan waters.

*W*aimānalo Beach skirts the base of the verdant Ko'olau Mountains.

$\mathcal{S}$oaring over 1,600 feet, Mount Olomana is named for a giant who legend says leaped from Kaua'i to make the peak his home.

$\mathcal{E}$xhilarating matches are scheduled at Waimānalo Polo Field from May through October.

$\mathcal{P}$alm tree–studded Waimānalo Beach Park is popular for picnicking.

Windward Oʻahu

WHERE NATURE REIGNS

In olden times, ʻohe (bamboo) forests blanketed the area called Kāneʻohe, which literally translates as "the bamboo man." The people who lived on this side of Oʻahu used the plant in many ways. It formed the framework for their thatched hale (houses); was carved into stamps for the decorating of kapa (tapa, or bark cloth); and was hollowed and filled with roasted kukui (candlenut tree) nuts to make torches. Spears were fashioned from the lightweight but durable bamboo, as were canoe outriggers, irrigation pipes, sled runners, knives, and "bottles" for storing drinking water. A favorite tale recounts how yet another use for the versatile ʻohe was discovered.

The majority of Kāneʻohe's population were farmers and fishermen who resided along its fertile shores. A few ʻeʻepa, or peculiar people, chose to dwell in the upland forests as poets and musicians. These mysterious

Today the towns of Kāneʻohe and Kailua are the hubs of the lush, lovely windward area—Oʻahu's Eden. Adorning this picturesque coast are ancient fishponds, beaches, parks, meadows, and forests alive with the intoxicating scents and vivid hues of a thousand different fruits, ferns, and flowers. With stunning vistas vying for attention in every direction, the windward coast of Oʻahu unabashedly displays the genius of Mother Nature.

Waters as warm and placid as a hot tub and sands as soft as baby powder make Kailua and Lanikai beaches irresistible diversions. Ranking among the most photogenic of Hawaiʻi's many

unexplored regions were thought to be sacred to the gods of nature, and parents prohibited their children from playing there, saying, "Do not go to those places or the Bamboo Man will keep you. We would miss you terribly if that happened."

But Hanoihu was a curious little boy who loved to explore. Unbeknownst to his parents, he would slip away and head to the forbidden upland sites whenever he could. His favorite playmate, a girl named Pū'ili, kept his secret well.

One day Hanoihu did not come home. Though the villagers made a long and diligent search, they could not find him and assumed he was dead. "The Bamboo Man must have taken him," they told the other children.

Pū'ili could not believe her friend was gone forever and set out to look for him in the upland forests. Once there, she could not believe this was a place her parents had taught her to fear. She was enthralled by its beauty—the ferns, flowers, trees, rippling streams, and above it all, a brilliant blue sky.

Byōdo-In Temple was dedicated on June 7, 1968, one hundred years to the day when the first Japanese immigrants arrived in Hawai'i.

Stretching two miles, Kailua Beach is one of the state's premier windsurfing spots. The adjacent 35-acre park provides barbecue facilities, a volleyball court, and tree-shaded picnic tables.

beaches, they are the perfect venues for windsurfing, bodysurfing, kayaking, and sailing. On weekends, savvy sun lovers arrive early to stake their spots on the sand.

Unique attractions add to the lure of the area. As serene as its surroundings, **Byōdo-In Temple** is a faithful replica of the nine-hundred-year-old temple of the same name located in Uji, Japan. Its meticulously maintained gardens, ponds teeming with koi, tree-lined pebble paths, and graceful gazebos and pagodas soothe the soul and invite meditation.

It's perpetually spring at Senator Fong's Plantation and Gardens. Every tropical plant and tree known to man seems to flourish in this 725-acre oasis, including rare sandalwood, twenty-five varieties of heliconia and ginger, and thirty types of palms. The garden's owner and namesake, Senator

PAGES 74–75:

Notes that sounded like the sweet chirping of a bird floated on a gentle breeze to her ears. Picking up two bamboo sticks, she clapped them together in time to the haunting music. Like magic, the melody led her to a waterfall-fed pool, where she saw Hanoihu sitting on the bank, blowing a bamboo pipe. Beside him was a tall, thin man who was waving his hands in rhythm with the notes.

Pū'ili was ecstatic about finding her friend, who introduced her to Kāne'ohe, the Bamboo Man, the inventor of the bamboo flute he was playing. "I shall name the flute after you," Kāne'ohe told the boy, "and the time-keeping sticks shall be named after your young companion. Now let's go back to the village, the three of us, where we can share our music with your friends and family." They went down the forest trail to the village, where they were greeted with great rejoicing and a huge feast.

And that is how the Hawaiians' bamboo instruments—the 'ohe hano ihu, *or nose flute, and the* pū'ili, *or rattle—came to be.*

*F*ormer Hawai'i Senator Hiram Fong enjoys tending the fruit trees and plants in his expansive garden.

*I*n the mid-1980s Kualoa Ranch shifted its focus from cattle raising to visitor activities such as trail rides into pristine Ka'a'awa Valley.

*H*ere's how the birds view Kāne'ohe Bay and the magnificent Ko'olau Range.

Hiram Fong, represented Hawai'i in Congress for seventeen years, beginning in 1959 when the Islands achieved statehood.

Once focused solely on cattle raising, Kualoa Ranch beefed up its business opportunities in 1985 by launching a recreational program geared toward visitors. Admirably, the ranch has expanded its activities in the great outdoors to include trail rides, dune cycling, hiking, target shooting, helicopter tours, snorkeling, kayaking, and scuba diving while preserving the pristine beauty of its pastureland, gardens, and beaches.

Providing a majestic backdrop to these captivating scenes are the Ko'olau Mountains, whose sheer fluted ramparts often are wreathed in mist and rainbows. Tucked along the foot of this verdant range are farms, ranches, and villages where change is a stranger and life is synchronized with the steady rhythm of nature.

*W*indsurfers' sails
are as bright as the
umbrellas that line
Kailua Beach.

A woman savors
the company of
the sun and sea at
Lanikai Beach.

*P*addlers navigate
past the Mokulua
islets by the light
of the moon.

A Kailua fisherman checks his net, hoping he'll find a good catch.

As night falls, paddlers bring their outrigger canoes back to their berths at Kailua Beach.

*S*unrise drapes a canopy of gold and orange behind the Mokulua islets.

*N*ight is equally dramatic here, especially when a full moon reigns.

*R*inged by the regal Ko'olaus, Kāne'ohe Bay is a lovely setting for water activities of all kinds.

The North Shore

COUNTRY LIVING

In steady rhythm, a woman of Kahuku sat beating fine strips of kapa *(tapa) on her handsome* kapa *log. She chanted as she beat the bark cloth, her voice in perfect harmony with the clear, sweet sound that the log emitted with each stroke.*

All day the woman pounded her kapa, *thoroughly enjoying what many others regarded to be a tedious task. When twilight finally came and erased the last rays of light from the sky, she reluctantly put away her work. She gathered the strips of* kapa *and placed them in a neat pile beside her beater to take home. But the log was too heavy to carry so, as she usually did, she pushed it into a hiding place among the ferns beside a spring.*

This day, though, she shoved the log a little too hard and it slipped over the wet foliage and into the spring. Although she ran her hands back and forth in the pool, the woman couldn't find the log. It had disappeared, possibly swept away by a strong underground current. If this was

Kahuku Point crowns O'ahu. The island's northernmost tip, it's a little more than an hour's drive from bustling Waikīkī but worlds away in terms of mood and ambience. On the North Shore it's country living, pure and simple. Time seems to tick more slowly here—and so does your heartbeat. There is no traffic, no noise, and there are no towering structures of steel and concrete. Unobstructed and unhindered, nature exuberantly shows off her beauty.

During the winter, monstrous swells thunder toward the shores of Waimea Bay, Sunset Beach, 'Ehukai, the Banzai Pipeline, and Chun's Reef. Prestigious surfing competitions with big-money purses are held at these sites each year, attracting hundreds

the case, the woman surmised the hidden stream would surface at some point and flow out to the ocean. She would find her log nearby, washed up on a bank.

At first light the next morning, she began following a stream, thinking it might connect to the one that had carried away her log. Even at that early hour, many of the women in her village were awake and beating their kapa, and she listened to the songs of the logs as she walked. Each log had its own distinctive voice. Some were low-pitched, some were high; others were loud, still others were muffled. None had the clear, sweet ring of her special log.

Her hunt yielded nothing. On and on she walked, farther and farther from her home. She followed many streams, thinking one would lead her to her log.

For four days she searched with no luck. Each night she was welcomed by friendly strangers and given food and a place to rest, but her hopes of finding her beloved log began to dim.

On the fifth day she saw an owl flying above her—a good omen. Farther down the trail she saw two more owls circling overhead. Another good sign! At last she came to the village of Waipahu, where she heard the music of many kapa beaters on logs. She paused and listened intently but could not pick out the unique sound of her log.

of photographers, sportswriters, and spectators who, with binoculars and cameras poised, marvel at the courage and daring acrobatics of champion wave riders from all around the world.

In olden times, villages and taro *lo'i* (irrigated terraces) dotted 1,800-acre Waimea Valley. Today, this lush, tranquil region is the home of Waimea Valley Audubon Center, which is managed by the National Audubon Society as a cultural, historical and natural resource. Here, visitors can enjoy quiet, contemplative activities that recall the Hawai'i of yesteryear, including strolling through beautiful gardens of native plants, hiking pristine trails, and viewing centuries-old living sites and agricultural terraces that have been carefully restored.

The Polynesian Cultural Center is your passport to the Pacific. Without boarding a plane, you can visit seven enchanting destinations in one day—Fiji, New Zealand, Samoa, Tahiti, Tonga, Hawai'i, and the Marquesas—and immerse yourself in their culture, history, and way of life. You can pound taro into poi

Then, all of a sudden, the beating ceased. The woman guessed the workers had taken a break to eat their midday meal. With the air now still, she heard the faint sounds of another log, coming from deep in the valley. At first she couldn't believe her ears; it was her log!

Up the trail she eagerly climbed toward the song of the kapa log. She rounded a turn on the path and came face-to-face with a woman beating kapa. The woman greeted her and invited her to share food and drink, but the traveler from Kahuku was more interested in the kapa log.

"I found it just this morning, lying beside the stream," said the kapa maker. "Doesn't it have a wonderful voice?"

"Yes," agreed the woman of Kahuku. "It sounds exactly like the log I lost five days ago. It slipped into a spring, and an undercurrent carried it away. I have been searching for it ever since."

"This must be your log," replied the other. "It has been carried here by water flowing underground all the way from Kahuku. What a miraculous journey! Surely the gods have a hand in this! Stay at my home tonight, and tomorrow you will be refreshed enough to take your log home."

And though it was a long journey back north to her home, the woman of Kahuku did not mind, for she had found her precious kapa log.

A Samoan youth at the Polynesian Cultural Center demonstrates how to squeeze milk from a fresh coconut.

Surfboards are as abundant as sunshine in Hale'iwa.

in the Hawaiian village, marvel as a Samoan youth deftly husks and cracks open a coconut, learn the hip-shaking Tahitian *tamure* dance, or watch Tongan women beat and decorate tapa. The essence of Polynesia is revealed through the work and amusements of its people.

Other North Shore attractions include Hale'iwa, a former sugar plantation town that's a curious mix of modest mom-and-pop stores and trendy boutiques, cafés, and art galleries. Shave ice in twenty different flavors—arguably the best on O'ahu—has made Matsumoto Store a Hale'iwa landmark. Meanwhile, gourmets may be surprised at the impressive selection of wines carried by unpretentious Fujioka Supermarket.

Simplicity with a splash of sass—that in a nutshell describes the charm of O'ahu's North Shore.

*T*he Polynesian Cultural Center allows you to tour the entire South Pacific without leaving Oʻahu.

*N*orth Shore residents offer bargain prices on bananas, papayas, pineapples, coconuts, and other produce at modest roadside stands.

A lone surfer surveys the conditions at Waimea Bay.

*D*aredevils defy nature at Waimea, where swells can top twenty feet during the winter months.

*T*he best wave riders in the world converge at Sunset Beach every year, hoping to win big money in big-name surfing competitions.

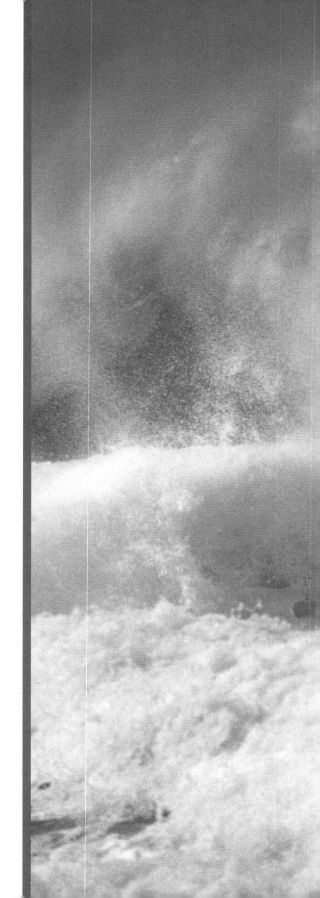

*S*urfers share an
appetite for thrills
and a special love
for the ocean.

*S*unsets are always
spectacular at
Sunset Beach.

About 6,000 species of tropical plants, shrubs and trees flourish at Waimea Valley Audubon Center. Many artifacts and archaeological sites have been documented. Since the National Audubon Society assumed management in June 2003, education about the park's history, culture and precious natural resources has been its primary focus.

*S*urfers wait
patiently for the
waves to reach
optimum heights
at Waimea Bay.

*D*uring the
summer Waimea
Bay exudes a
tranquil air.

*H*ale'iwa high-
lights: pareus
in a vivid palette of
colors, refreshing
shave ice, eye-
catching art,
trendy cafés
and shops, and
surfboards galore.

103

*F*ields of pineapple
and sugarcane still
flourish in Waialua.

Leeward O'ahu

THE SUN COAST

Basking in the constant embrace of the sun, Ka'ena, the westernmost tip of O'ahu, appropriately means "the heat, red-hot, or glowing." Indeed, few sunsets are as spectacular as those that unfold before the hot, dry shores of Ka'ena Point.

It was here in a stark landscape of sand dunes, wild vegetation, and wind- and surf-pummeled cliffs that Māui, the heroic demigod, is said to have pondered a way to make travel between O'ahu and Kaua'i easier. Ka'ena Point was the nearest anchorage for canoes traveling from Kaua'i, some one hundred miles across usually choppy seas to the northwest. What if he hauled Kaua'i over the ocean to O'ahu with his magical fishhook and a strong rope woven of 'ie'ie vines? If he could join Kaua'i with O'ahu, it would no longer be necessary for people to embark on a slow, strenuous canoe journey across the restless Kaua'i Channel.

Mom and kids relish quiet time at Mākaha Beach.

Life along the Wai'anae coast is simple and peaceful.

The craggy Wai'anae Range separates leeward O'ahu (stretching twenty-two miles from Ka'ena Point to Kalaeloa) from the flat central portion of the island that's still dominated by fields of pineapple and sugarcane. In the northern sector of the range, Mount Ka'ala, O'ahu's highest peak, rises 4,020 feet above sea level. In its shadow, in sharp contrast to the cool blue of the ocean, lie the arid acres of the Wai'anae Coast.

This area, which claims the largest percentage of native Hawaiians on O'ahu, has undergone major changes in recent decades. To the south, Kapolei, the island's "second city," is sprouting up, complete with subdivisions, a business district, schools, and parks.

FACING PAGE:
"Mākaha" means fierce, and this is exactly how the ocean can be during winter. That, however, doesn't discourage intrepid surfers. International surfing competitions have been held here since 1952.

From remote, rugged Ka'ena Point, Māui cast his fishhook and rope across the channel and latched onto Kaua'i. He pulled and pulled with all his might, but he only could loosen a boulder at the base of the island's sea cliffs. The huge rock fell from Māui's fishhook into the waters off Ka'ena Point, where it still can be seen today. Though his efforts were valiant, Māui could not budge the rest of Kaua'i, and so it remains a separate gem sparkling in the vast Pacific.

In addition to easing traffic and population density concerns in urban Honolulu, part of the vision for Kapolei was to establish West O'ahu as a mecca for visitors, a world-class alternative to Waikīkī. Swank Kō 'Olina Resort presently encompasses a luxury hotel and a championship golf course, and just a few miles away, the amazing slides, rivers, mega pools, and other diversions at Hawaiian Waters Adventure Park, the state's newest attraction, draw hundreds each day for hours of splashy fun.

In ancient times, fishermen trolling the waters between Nānākuli and Ka'ena Point were rewarded with a bounty of tasty delicacies. These days most people venturing into the ocean there are intrepid wave riders hoping to conquer the colossal swells that roil off the coast, reaching heights of more than thirty feet during the winter. Be aware: this is no place for novices. Expert surfers pair with the magnificent waves of Mākaha (which translates as "fierce") and Yokohama Bay in a dance that is at once breathtaking and perilous.

Desolate Ka'ena Point lies at the westernmost tip of the island.

The last stretch of sand in leeward O'ahu unfolds at Keawa'ula Bay. Japanese immigrants who came from Yokohama to work in the cane fields often fished along this shore. Thus the area became known as Yokohama Bay.

*T*he craggy Wai'anae Range hugs the leeward coastline.

*M*ā'ili Beach (below) disappears in the high winter surf, but in the calm of summer it's pleasant for sunning and swimming.

*S*ummer blesses Mākaha Beach (facing page) with abundant sand and inviting waters.

$\mathcal{Y}$ouths race
their outrigger
canoes in Mākaha's
lively waves.

*B*lue skies crown Wai'anae Valley.

*D*ating back to the seventeenth century, Kāne'ākī Heiau (a place of worship) was dedicated to Lono, the Hawaiian god of harvest and fertility. Bishop Museum directed the restoration of its lava rock walls; the spirit tower and *ki'i* (religious image) are replicas.

*W*ai‘anae Harbor;
the luxurious JW
Marriott ‘Ihilani
Resort and Spa;
Kō ‘Olina Golf
Course; and Kapolei,
O‘ahu's "second city."

*T*he four man-
made lagoons
adjacent to ‘Ihilani
Resort are alluring
venues for relaxation
and recreation.

References

Bell, Brian, ed. *Insight Guides: Hawaii.* Singapore: APA Publications, 1998.

Bisignani, J. D. *Honolulu–Waikiki Handbook.* Chico, Calif.: Moon Publications, 1995.

Foster, Jeanette, and Jocelyn Fujii. *Frommer's '99 Hawaii.* New York: Simon and Schuster, 1998.

Paki, Pilahi. *Legends of Hawaii: Oahu's Yesterday.* Honolulu: Victoria Publishers, 1972.

Pūkuʻi, Mary Kawena, comp. *Tales of the Menehune.* Honolulu: Kamehameha Schools Press, 1994.

———. *The Water of Kāne and Other Legends of the Hawaiian Islands.* Honolulu: Kamehameha Schools Press, 1994.